HARRY POTTER AND THE CHAMBER OF SECRETS

by
J.K. Rowling

Student Packet

Written by
Elizabeth Klar and Cheryl Klar-Trim

Y0-DYU-465

Contains masters for:

2 Prereading Activities
1 Study Guide (11 pages)
12 Vocabulary Activities
2 Critical Thinking Activities
3 Literary Analysis Activities
2 Writing Activities
2 Comprehension Quizzes
1 Novel Unit Test (6 pages)
Plus Detailed Answer Key

Note

The hardcover edition published by Scholastic Press, ©1998 by J.K. Rowling, was used to prepare this guide. The page numbers may differ in other editions of the novel.

Please note: Please assess the appropriateness of this book for the age level and maturity of your students prior to reading and discussing it with your class.

ISBN 1-58130-655-5

To order, contact your local school supply store, or—

Novel Units, Inc.
P.O. Box 791610
San Antonio, TX 78279

Name _____

The main character in a story is called the protagonist. Sometimes we call the protagonist the hero or heroine (the "good" person). The character that opposes the hero in a story is called the antagonist. Sometimes we call the antagonist the villain (the "bad" person).

Directions: Think about stories you have read. Who were some of the protagonists (heroes/heroines) in these stories? Who were the antagonists (villains)? List some of the protagonists and antagonists and the stories in which they appeared.

Story	Protagonists	Antagonists

Complete the chart below by listing some common characteristics of protagonists and antagonists. For example, a protagonist is often brave. An antagonist may be sly or cruel. Sometimes the antagonist is not just a person but a belief or custom.

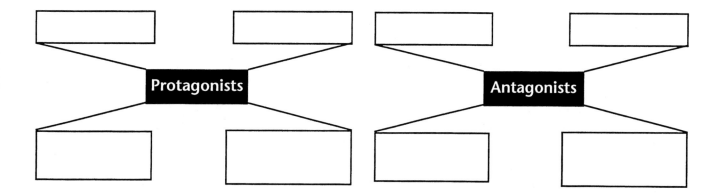

As you read *Harry Potter and the Chamber of Secrets,* decide who is the protagonist and who or what is the antagonist. Notice their characteristics and compare/contrast them to the characters you listed in the chart above.

Name _____

Directions: Think about each idea listed below, then freewrite about each idea. Try to write about each idea for at least 5 minutes. Use extra paper if you need it. Be prepared to discuss your thoughts with classmates.

1. bully

2. orphan

3. strong-willed

4. friendship

5. bravery

Name _____

Directions: Write a brief answer to each study question as you read the novel at home or in class. Use the questions to guide your reading and prepare for class discussion.

Chapter One, The Worst Birthday

1. What statement does Harry make to Dudley at the breakfast table that makes Uncle Vernon so angry?
2. Where does Harry attend school?
3. What does Harry miss about Hogwarts School?
4. What mark does Harry have on his forehead?
5. What is Harry supposed to do during the dinner party?
6. What does Mr. Dursley plan to do if he closes the big business deal at dinner?
7. How does Harry feel on his twelfth birthday?
8. Why doesn't Harry use his owl, Hedwig, to send messages to his friends?
9. What does Harry see in the hedges?
10. How does Mrs. Dursley punish Harry for teasing Dudley?
11. What does Mrs. Dursley give Dudley to eat after he finishes his work?

Chapter Two, Dobby's Warning

1. Who did Harry see staring at him through the hedges?
2. What does Dobby look like?
3. What is Dobby wearing when he meets Harry?
4. What is Dobby?
5. How does Dobby react when Harry asks him to sit down?
6. What does Dobby warn Harry against doing?
7. What happened to all the letters Harry's friends sent to him during the summer?
8. What does Dobby do to get Harry in trouble?
9. How is the letter from the Ministry of Magic delivered to Harry?
10. Why is Mr. Dursley no longer afraid of Harry's magic?
11. What does Mr. Dursley do to Harry after he reads the letter from the Ministry of Magic?
12. What does Harry dream about as he is locked in his room?
13. Who does Harry see staring at him through the bars in his window?

© Novel Units, Inc.

5

Chapter Three, The Burrow

1. What is Ron riding in when he gets to Harry's house?
2. How does Ron know that Harry received a warning letter from the Ministry of Magic?
3. How is Harry able to get his wand, broomstick, and other Hogwarts stuff?
4. What awakens Mr. Dursley while Harry is escaping?
5. How is Harry able to escape from Mr. Dursley's grasp?
6. Why does Harry let Hedwig out of her cage as he flies off in the car?
7. What does Harry yell out to the Dursleys as he flies away in the car?
8. Who is Lucius Malfoy and whom does he support?
9. Who is Errol?
10. What department does Ron's dad work in at the Ministry of Magic?
11. Does Mrs. Weasley praise or scold her boys when they arrive home from Harry's?
12. Who runs into the kitchen and squeals at the sight of Harry?
13. What does Mrs. Weasley ask her sons to do to the garden?
14. What do the gnomes yell as the boys try to rid them from the garden?
15. What does Mr. Weasley say he found on his nine raids?

Chapter Four, At Flourish and Blotts

1. What does the mirror over the kitchen mantelpiece shout to Harry?
2. What does Harry find unusual at Ron's house?
3. What does Mrs. Weasley try to force Harry to do?
4. Who is the author of most of the books on Harry's school reading list?
5. Who does Percy accidentally sit on during breakfast?
6. In her letter to Ron and Harry, what does Hermione say she is busy doing?
7. What activities are Bill and Charlie, Ron's older brothers, involved in?
8. How does Harry travel from Ron's house to Diagon Alley?
9. Who, from his school, does Harry see at Borgin and Burkes?
10. Who does Harry meet on Knockturn Alley?
11. What does Hagrid tell Harry he was looking for on Knockturn Alley?
12. By what means are customers taken to their vaults in Gringotts Bank?

13. What is the name of the book Percy is found reading?

14. What announcement does Gilderoy Lockhart make at Flourish and Blotts?

15. What does Harry do with the books Gilderoy Lockhart gives him?

16. Who does Mr. Weasley fight with? Who breaks up the fight?

Chapter Five, The Whomping Willow

1. How do George and Fred celebrate the night before they return to school?

2. How is Mr. Weasley able to fit six large trunks into his car?

3. What is so tricky about getting to platform nine and three-quarters?

4. Why do Ron and Harry miss their train?

5. How do Ron and Harry get to school?

6. Why don't Ron's parents need the car to get home?

7. Do Ron and Harry make a grand entrance at school like they hoped? How do they actually land?

8. What is special about the tree Ron crashes into?

9. What is happening in the great hall when Ron and Harry arrive?

10. According to Snape, why are Ron and Harry featured in the Evening Prophet?

11. What does Professor McGonagall say Harry and Ron should have done when they could not get through the barrier at the train station?

12. How are Harry and Ron punished?

13. What is the new password for Gryffindor Hall?

Chapter Six, Gilderoy Lockhart

1. What is a Howler?

2. Who receives a Howler at breakfast, and what is it about?

3. What have Professor Sprout and Gilderoy Lockhart just finished doing when they meet the students by the greenhouse?

4. What advice does Lockhart give Harry about his fame?

5. What is special about the Mandrake plant?

6. Why is the Mandrake plant dangerous?

7. What does Colin Creevey want Harry to do?

8. How is the situation between Malfoy and Harry resolved?

9. What is Lockhart's secret ambition?

10. How do the pixies affect the class?

Chapter Seven, Mudbloods and Murmurs

1. What happens to Ron's wand in Charms class?

2. What does Harry explain to Colin as they walk to the Quidditch field?

3. What position does Harry play on the Quidditch team?

4. Who interrupts the Gryffindor team as they begin to practice?

5. Who is the new seeker on the Slytherin team?

6. What did Lucius Malfoy buy for the Slytherin team?

7. What does Ron cough up after being hit by his own wand?

8. Where do Harry and Hermione take Ron for help?

9. Who is leaving Hagrid's house when Ron, Harry, and Hermione arrive?

10. What is a Mudblood?

11. What is Hagrid growing for the Halloween feast?

12. What chores are Ron and Harry assigned for detention?

13. What happens to Harry as he is addressing Veronica Smethley's letter?

Chapter Eight, The Deathday Party

1. Which ghost does Harry meet in the corridor?

2. Who gets upset with Harry for tracking mud into the hall?

3. Who is Peeves?

4. What does Harry find in Filch's office?

5. Who convinces Peeves to destroy the cabinet to distract Filch?

6. What event does Nearly Headless Nick invite Harry to attend?

7. What does Moaning Myrtle haunt in Gryffindor Hall?

8. What was the food like at Nick's party?

9. How does Peeves' appearance differ from the rest of the ghosts?

10. What does Harry hear in the passageway as he is leaving Nick's party?

11. What do Harry, Ron, and Hermione find while Harry tries to follow the menacing voice?

Chapter Nine, The Writing on the Wall

1. How does Filch react when he sees Mrs. Norris hanging from the torch basket?

2. Is Mrs. Norris really dead?

3. What kind of spell does Dumbledore think has been placed on Mrs. Norris?

4. What does Dumbledore think will cure Mrs. Norris?

5. How does Snape want to punish Harry for hanging the cat?

6. What is a Squib?

7. Why is Ginny upset about Mrs. Norris?

8. Why does Hermione want a copy of *Hogwarts, A History*?

9. Who tells Harry the legend of the Chamber of Secrets?

10. What is the horror in the Chamber of Secrets?

11. Who do some of the students at Hogwarts suspect is the Heir of Slytherin?

12. What does Ron see in the corridor that frightens him?

13. Who does the trio see in the girls' bathroom?

14. Who does Harry suspect is the Heir of Slytherin?

15. What is Polyjuice?

Chapter Ten, The Rogue Bludger

1. Which teacher does Hermione get to sign authorization for a book in the restricted section of the library?

2. Where do Ron, Hermione, and Harry go for privacy while reading the *Moste Potente Potions* book?

3. Which ingredients of Polyjuice does Hermione think will be hard to get?

4. What does Hermione think is worse than brewing up a difficult potion?

5. How long is it going to take to make the Polyjuice?

6. What color are the Gryffindor Quidditch robes?

7. What attacks Harry during the Quidditch game?

8. How does Harry break his arm?

9. Who tries to fix Harry's broken arm?

10. What affect does Lockhart's spell have on Harry's broken arm?

11. What affect does the Skele-Gro have on Harry?

12. Who does Harry discover is responsible for stopping the barrier from letting him and Ron through at the train station?

13. Who is responsible for making the Bludger go after Harry?

14. Who do McGonagall and Dumbledore bring into the ward as Harry is recovering? What happened to this person?

Chapter Eleven, The Dueling Club

1. Where do Ron and Hermione go to start the Polyjuice?

2. How do Fred and George try to cheer up Ginny after Colin is Petrified?

3. What do Ron, Hermione, and Harry plan to do at school during the Christmas break?

4. What does Harry use to distract Snape so Hermione can steal the needed ingredients for the Polyjuice?

5. Who gives a dueling demonstration in the Great Hall?

6. What do the professors use to duel instead of swords?

7. Who is Harry paired with to practice dueling?

8. What is Parselmouth?

9. What is the "mark of a Dark wizard"?

10. What do the Hufflepuff students think is the reason Harry survived the attack from "You-Know-Who" when he was a baby?

11. Who does Harry find Petrified in the corridor?

Chapter Twelve, The Polyjuice Potion

1. What kind of hat is in Dumbledore's office?

2. What does the Sorting Hat tell Harry about Slytherin?

3. Why kind of bird does Dumbledore have?

4. What does Dumbledore tell Harry are the special things a phoenix can do?

5. Does Dumbledore think Harry is responsible for the attacks?

6. What does Ron think is the reason Draco Malfoy is giving Harry sour looks?

7. Who do Mr. and Mrs. Weasley visit during Christmas? Where do they go?

8. What does Harry receive as a Christmas gift from the Dursleys?

9. Who does Hermione plan to turn into using the Polyjuice?

10. How long will it take for the Polyjuice potion to wear off?

11. What does the Goyle-laced Polyjuice potion taste like? What does is look like?

12. What is the Slytherin password?

13. What is the "funny thing" that Malfoy shows Ron and Harry when they are disguised as Goyle and Crabbe?

14. What is Azkaban?

Chapter Thirteen, The Very Secret Diary

1. Why does Madam Pomfrey place curtains around Hermione's bed?

2. Which teacher sends Hermione a "get well" card?

3. What makes Moaning Myrtle cry?

4. How old is the diary Ron and Harry find?

5. Whose name is in the diary?

6. Why does Harry suspect T. M. Riddle is Muggle-born?

7. What does Hermione suspect T. M. Riddle may have done 50 years ago?

8. What does Madam Pomfrey tell Filch is a sign that the Mandrakes are leaving childhood?

9. What is Gilderoy Lockhart's "moral booster"?

10. Who takes the diary from Harry during the singing telegram disturbance?

11. What odd thing does Harry notice about the diary when he reaches Flitwick's class?

12. How is Harry able to communicate with the diary?

13. What does Harry discover about Tom's parents?

14. Through the use of Tom's diary, who does Harry discover is responsible for opening the Chamber of Secrets 50 years earlier?

Chapter Fourteen, Cornelius Fudge

1. Who was Fluffy?

2. Why do Ron, Harry, and Hermione decide not to talk to Hagrid about why he was expelled?

3. How will Professor Sprout be able to tell when the Mandrakes are fully mature?

4. What does Harry think is the only thing at school he is really good at?

5. What is stolen from Harry's room?

6. Which two students are victims of the double attack before the Hufflepuff and Gryffindor Quidditch match?

7. What does Professor McGonagall find lying next to the two victims?

8. What is the only thing Harry inherited from his father?

9. How do Ron and Harry get to Hagrid's without being seen?

10. Who comes to see Hagrid while Ron and Harry are hiding in the corner in Hagrid's house?

11. Where does the Minister of Magic want to take Hagrid?

12. Does Dumbledore believe that Hagrid is responsible for the attacks?

13. What news does Malfoy bring to Dumbledore?

14. What does Hagrid claim will happen if Dumbledore is removed as headmaster?

15. What clue does Hagrid shout to Harry and Ron as he is taken away?

Chapter Fifteen, Aragog

1. How does Harry feel about being shepherded to and from classes?

2. Which student seems to be enjoying the atmosphere of terror and suspicion?

3. Who does Draco Malfoy want to replace Dumbledore as headmaster?

4. Where do Ron and Harry think the spiders they spot in the greenhouse are headed?

5. What does Harry claim are some of the good things in the Forbidden Forrest?

6. Why is the Gryffindor common room so crowded?

7. Why do Harry and Ron leave the Invisibility Cloak at Hagrid's house?

8. What happens when Harry takes out his wand and murmurs "Lumos"? Why doesn't Ron do this too?

9. How does the flying car behave towards Harry and Ron when they find it in the forest?

10. Who is Aragog?

11. What is the reason Aragog says he never attacked humans?

12. Where is Aragog from?

13. How are Harry and Ron able to escape from the giant spiders?

14. What does Ron say is Hagrid's problem with monsters?

15. Who does Harry suspect is the girl who was killed by the monster 50 years earlier?

Chapter Sixteen, The Chamber of Secrets

1. Who tells the students that they will have exams in June?
2. What good news does Professor McGonagall give the students?
3. Who is about to reveal forbidden information to Harry?
4. Who interrupts Ginny as she is about to tell Harry a secret?
5. Who finds Harry and Ron standing in the hall alone?
6. Where do the boys tell Professor McGonagall they are going?
7. What does Harry find in Hermione's hand?
8. What single word does Harry find written beneath the library article?
9. Why does Harry hear the serpent talk and no one else?
10. What kind of animal flees when the Basilisk comes near?
11. How does the serpent move through the castle?
12. Where are the boys going to meet Professor McGonagall?
13. Where do Harry and Ron hide when they hear that all teachers are to report to the staff room?
14. What information does Professor McGonagall give to the teachers?
15. What teacher leaves the staff meeting in a hurry?
16. Who do Harry and Ron think will help them get into the Chamber of Secrets?
17. What is Lockhart doing in his classroom?
18. Does Lockhart tell the truth when he writes about his adventures in his textbooks?
19. What is the last thing Moaning Myrtle remembered before she died?
20. How does Harry open the door to the Chamber of Secrets?
21. What is Lockhart going to tell the teachers when he leaves Harry and Ron in the Chamber of Secrets?
22. What happens to Ron's wand as Lockhart waves it in the air?
23. What does Harry do when he finds himself separated from Lockhart and Ron?

Chapter Seventeen, The Heir of Slytherin

1. What does Harry worry about as he stands at the end of the dimly-lit chamber?
2. What does Harry see as he walks between the serpentine columns?
3. How did Tom Riddle look as he spoke to Harry?

4. What did Tom say he was when Harry asked if he was a ghost?

5. What are some things that Ginny wrote in the diary?

6. Why does Ginny try to dispose of the diary?

7. Who sees through Tom Riddle's deception?

8. What question does Tom want Harry to answer?

9. Who does Tom Riddle say that he is?

10. What makes Tom whirl around and stare down the empty Chamber?

11. What emerged from the flames that erupted at the top of the nearest pillar?

12. Where did the phoenix go when it landed in the Chamber?

13. What did the phoenix drop at Harry's feet?

14. Why did Harry's mother die?

15. What does Tom want to do to teach Harry a lesson?

16. How are Tom and Harry alike?

17. What is coming out of the statue's mouth as Tom speaks to Slytherin?

18. Who attacks the Basilisk?

19. What damage does the phoenix do to the Basilisk?

20. What falls out of the Sorting Hat?

21. How does Fawkes, the phoenix, save Harry from the poisonous fang in his arm?

22. How does Harry defeat Tom Riddle?

23. What happens as Tom leaves the Chamber?

24. What happened to Lockhart when he used Ron's wand?

25. Who helps Harry, Ron, Ginny, and Lockhart through the tunnel?

Chapter Eighteen, Dobby's Reward

1. Who is crying in Professor McGonagall's office? Why?

2. Where does Fawkes go as he flies past Harry?

3. What enchanted Ginny?

4. Where did Ginny find the diary?

5. Is there any lasting harm done to Hermione?

6. What is Professor McGonagall's first name?

7. Does Dumbledore expel Harry and Ron for breaking the school rules?

8. Does Lockhart recognize his name as Dumbledore addresses him? Why not?

9. Where does Ron take Lockhart?

10. What is the first thing that Dumbledore tells Harry when they are finally alone?

11. How does Harry get the gift of Parseltongue?

12. What makes Harry different from Riddle?

13. What does Dumbledore say only a true Gryffindor could do?

14. What does Dumbledore say that Harry needs?

15. Who comes through the door before Harry can make it to the feast?

16. Who comes with Lucius Malfoy?

17. Who is pointing to the diary and then to Malfoy?

18. Who gave the diary to Ginny? How?

19. How does Harry give the diary back to Malfoy?

20. What happens to Dobby as Malfoy tosses him Harry's sock?

21. What does Harry ask Dobby to do?

22. What did the teachers do when Dumbledore made the announcement that Lockhart would not be returning next school year?

23. What did Ginny see Percy doing, that he didn't want anyone to know about?

24. What does Harry ask Ron to do as he leaves for summer vacation?

© Novel Units, Inc.

15

Name _____

Chapter One

irritably (2)	incredible (2)	abnormality (2)	dormitory (3)
cauldron (3)	sorcerer (4)	graciously (5)	rapturously (5)
toneless (6)	emerged (6)	arch-enemy (8)	cunning (8)
livid (8)	jeering (8)	sneered (9)	lolled (10)
savagely (10)	loin (10)	whisked (10)	

Directions: Write each vocabulary word on a slip of paper (one word per piece). Using the circle below, make a spinner. Play the following game with a classmate. (It is a good idea to have a dictionary and thesaurus handy.) Place the papers in a small container. The first player draws a word from the container. The player then spins the spinner and follows the direction where the pointer lands. For example, if the player draws the word "livid" and lands on "define," the player must define the word livid. If the player's partner accepts the answer as correct, the first player scores 1 point and play passes to the second player. If the player's partner challenges the answer, the first player uses a dictionary or thesaurus to prove the answer is correct. If the player can prove the answer is correct, the player earns 2 points. If the player cannot prove the answer is correct, the opposing player earns 2 points. Play continues until all the words have been used. The player with the most points wins.

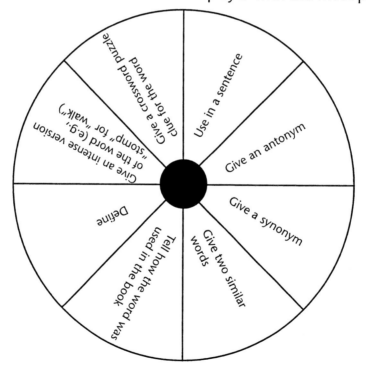

Directions: Choose 10 vocabulary words from the list. On your own paper, write a sentence for each word, but replace each vocabulary word with a phrase. Give your sentences to a classmate who will replace each phrase with the correct vocabulary word from the list.

Chapter Two

falter (13)	ushered (13)	adoration (13)	wails (15)
distinctly (15)	rubbish (15)	reverently (15)	orb-like (15)
grubby (15)	valiant (16)	chink (16)	bounded (17)
slyly (18)	nimbly (18)	lurching (19)	igid (20)
gloss (20)	banshee (20)	lunatics (20)	demonic (20)
brandishing (20)	expel (21)	maniac (21)	relenting (22)
ruffled (22)	grimly (22)	goggled (23)	

Directions: Think about the characters listed below. Write each vocabulary word under the character you associate with that word. You have three more words than you need to fill in all of the boxes. (There may be more than one way to sort the words. Be prepared to support your decisions about where words belong.)

Harry	Ron	Malfoy

On another sheet of paper, write a paragraph about one of the characters listed in the chart. The paragraph should include at least half of the words you listed under that character's name.

Chapter Three

revved (25)	hoisted (25)	snatched (27)	scrambling (27)
bellow (27)	dumbstruck (28)	soared (28)	fiasco (28)
dodgy (28)	craning (29)	dung (29)	manors (29)
collapsed (30)	berserk (31)	peering (31)	patchwork (31)
perched (32)	lopsided (32)	jumble (32)	jaunty (33)
cowered (33)	prodding (33)	hoarse (33)	cramped (33)
clattering (34)	haphazardly (34)	flicked (34)	diversion (35)
undertone (35)	wretched (35)	audible (36)	woe (36)
slouched (36)	gnarled (36)	peony (36)	straggling (37)
ferrets (38)	poker (38)	loophole (39)	faltered (39)
ajar (40)	plaque (40)	emblazoned (40)	spawn (40)

Directions: Select ten vocabulary words from above. Create a crossword puzzle answer key by filling in the grid below. Be sure to number the squares for each word. Blacken any spaces not used by the letters. Then, write clues to the crossword puzzle. Number the clues to match the numbers in the squares. The teacher will give each student a blank grid. Make a blank copy of your crossword puzzle for other students to answer. Exchange your clues with someone else and solve the blank puzzle he/she gives you. Check the completed puzzles with the answer keys.

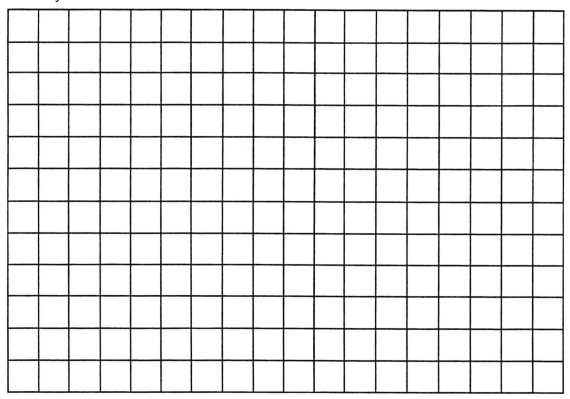

Name _____

Chapter Four

bombard (42)	porridge (43)	prone (43)	emerged (43)
parchment (43)	peered (44)	elder (44)	moulting (44)
paddock (45)	gloated (46)	vault (46)	soot (48)
fidget (48)	whirl (49)	gingerly (49)	dimly (49)
withered (49)	hearth (49)	quelling (50)	prudent (50)
presume (51)	meddlesome (51)	surge (51)	abashed (52)
haggle (52)	coil (52)	dingy (53)	leered (54)
bristling (54)	croaked (54)	scruff (54)	apothecary (54)
mopped (55)	frantic (55)	enviously (55)	indignantly (56)
vaguely (57)	quill (57)	clamoring (58)	undertone (58)
autobiography (58)	wafting (60)	limelight (61)	sneer (61)
retorted (61)	amid (62)	flushed (62)	apprehensively (62)
thrust (63)	beckoned (63)	brawling (63)	subdued (63)

Directions: Write a vocabulary word in each box below. The word should correspond to the column's category.

Noun	Verb	Adjective or Adverb
♣	✿	✛
❖	✾	❋
✛	✽	✾
♦	♣	▲
✾	♦	❖
✽	▲	✿
▲	✛	♦
✿	❋	♣
❋	❖	✽

Find sets of words with the same symbols. For example, the three words written besides the ✿ form a set. On a separate sheet of paper, write a sentence that includes each set of words.

Chapter Five

conjured (65)	sumptuous (65)	reckoned (66)	trundled (66)
clambered (66)	briskly (67)	wedged (67)	barrier (69)
vain (69)	cavernous (70)	ignition (70)	pummeled (70)
fabulous (71)	turrets (70)	toffees (70)	moors (72)
croaked (72)	accelerator (72)	whine (72)	cajolingly (73)
billowing (74)	limply (74)	lurching (75)	python (75)
tether (75)	sprawled (75)	ejecting (75)	brandishing (76)
snort (76)	flailing (76)	innumerable (76)	hovering (76)
goblets (76)	bespectacled (77)	frayed (77)	petrified (77)
mousy-haired (77)	aquamarine (77)	sarcastic (77)	barrier (78)
walloped (79)	fetch (79)	flinched (80)	ominously (80)
grave (80)	flouted (81)	tart (82)	venom (82)
wrathful (82)	piercing (82)	detention (82)	lecture (84)
marathon (84)	scarlet (85)	nudged (85)	spiral (85)
scowl (85)	awestruck (85)		

Directions: Your teacher will divide the class into two teams, giving each team a stack of notecards with vocabulary words on them. A member of team # 1 will look at a card and read it silently. Then he/she will go in front of the class and pantomime the vocabulary word. Team #2 will try to guess the vocabulary word. The teams take turns acting out vocabulary words for each other. The teacher will assign points each time a vocabulary word is guessed correctly. Continue with the game until all cards have been used. After the game, collect the cards and put them in a stack. Each member of the team should then draw a vocabulary card from the stack and write a sentence using the word. Share your sentences with the class.

conjured

Name _____

Chapter Six

tureens (86)	kippers (86)	bedraggled (87)	deafening (88)
swiveling (88)	crimson (88)	inquiry (88)	stunned (88)
tidal wave (88)	babble (88)	dwell (89)	twinge (89)
squat (89)	immaculate (89)	exotic (90)	disgruntled (90)
trestle (91)	restorative (92)	antidotes (92)	compost (93)
gnashed (94)	traipsed (94)	scuttled (95)	engulfed (95)
volley (95)	flanked (97)	thuggish (97)	cronies (97)
sniggering (97)	menacing (97)	jovially (98)	humiliation (98)
smirking (98)	paternally (98)	chortle (98)	roguish (100)
rapt (100)	foulest (101)	cowering (101)	blighters (101)
bizarre (102)	pandemonium (102)	rampaging (102)	

Directions: Use three words from the vocabulary list in an original sentence about each of the following characters from the story. Use a different set of words for each character.

1. Ron _____

_____

2. Hermione _____

_____

3. Gilderoy Lockhart _____

_____

4. Professor Sprout _____

_____

5. Harry _____

_____

6. Malfoy _____

_____

Now rewrite each sentence, but add one more word from the list. Write your new sentences on the back of this paper.

Chapter Seven

exasperated (104)　malfunctioning (104)　burly (105)　bemusedly (106)
remnants (109)　magnified (109)　smugly (112)　threshold (114)
plunking (114)　squelchily (115)　magenta (116)　genially (117)
loathed (119)　slouched (119)　scalawag (119)　prattle (120)

Chapter Eight

spate (122)　squelched (123)　morosely (123)　torrential (123)
tartan (125)　jowls (125)　aquiver (125)　manacles (125)
havoc (126)　intrigued (127)　pouchy (128)　rejection (129)
dignified (129)　tenterhooks (130)　keenly (130)　emitting (131)
bellowing (131)　quavering (132)　tantrums (133)　salvers (133)
putrid (133)　glummest (134)　lank (134)　pelting (135)
podium (136)　lamented (136)　phantom (137)　daubed (138)
immobile (139)

Directions: Choose a total of 15 words from the vocabulary lists in Chapters Seven and Eight. On a separate sheet of paper, make a word map (like the one shown below) for each word.

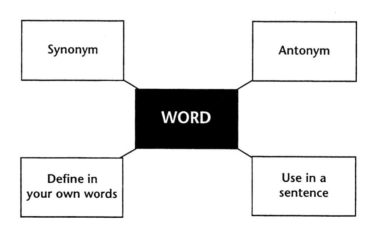

Name _____

Chapter Nine

blotched (142)	restorative (144)	snigger (145)	blanched (146)
abruptly (147)	bickering (148)	varied (148)	drone (148)
stupor (148)	ludicrous (149)	precise (150)	blearily (150)
pursing (150)	obscured (150)	arrant (151)	verifiable (152)
teeming (152)	bustle (157)		

Chapter Ten

reconstructions (161)	yeti (161)	revolted (163)	dedicate (163)
eradication (163)	forgery (164)	barricaded (164)	leaden (167)
pelted (168)	tampered (169)	forfeit (170)	rogue (170)
midair (171)	remotely (173)	mended (173)	inept (174)
distract (175)	heed (176)	flogging (176)	enslavement (177)
grievously (177)	dregs (178)	stammered (178)	meddle (178)
noble (179)	valiant (179)	quivering (179)	urgent (179)
cardigan (179)	wrenched (180)	rigid (180)	acrid (180)
shadowy (181)			

Directions: Write summaries on the chapters titled "The Writing on the Wall" and "The Rogue Bludger." Use at least 10 words from the corresponding vocabulary list in each summary.

Chapter Nine _____

_____

_____

_____

_____

Chapter Ten _____

_____

_____

_____

_____

Chapter Eleven

clumsily (182)	portable (183)	foul (184)	triumphant (184)
leeches (184)	ventured (185)	apoplectic (185)	talisman (185)
amulets (185)	newt (185)	legendary (186)	loomed (186)
diversion (186)	mayhem (186)	retaliated (186)	prod (187)
lumbered (187)	frothed (188)	resplendent (189)	sportingly (189)
irritably (190)	tottering (190)	smirking (191)	vague (192)
ashen-faced (192)	skittering (192)	flustered (193)	devastation (193)
cuffed (194)	brandished (194)	casters (194)	docile (194)
ominous (195)	egging (196)	descendant (197)	pummeling (197)
fretted (197)	bandy (198)	reproving (200)	gilded (200)
balaclava (201)	waft (204)	gargoyle (204)	

Chapter Twelve

spindle-legged (205)	emitting (205)	decrepit (206)	balefully (206)
feverishly (207)	smoulder (207)	phoenix (207)	immensely (207)
penetrating (208)	ranting (208)	disembodied (209)	stampede (209)
skirting (209)	ludicrous (210)	pompously (211)	surge (212)
bout (212)	goblet (212)	sniggering (212)	comeuppance (213)
stupefied (213)	lurked (214)	trifle (214)	ecstatically (214)
sprinted (215)	glutinous (215)	tumblers (215)	sluggishly (215)
splotched (215)	dollops (215)	frothed (216)	writhing (216)
morosely (217)	indistinguishable (217)	bizarre (218)	labyrinthine (219)
derisive (220)	elaborately (221)	silhouetted (221)	scornfully (222)
contorted (222)	sacked (222)	bated (223)	petulantly (223)
relish (223)	hoist (225)		

Directions: Choose 15 vocabulary words from the lists above. Write the words on the numbered lines below.

1. _____   2. _____   3. _____

4. _____   5. _____   6. _____

7. _____   8. _____   9. _____

10. _____   11. _____   12. _____

13. _____   14. _____   15. _____

Next, use each of the following sets of words in an original sentence. Your sentences should show that you know the meanings of the vocabulary words as they are used in the story.

Sentence 1: words 1 and 7   Sentence 6: words 12 and 10

Sentence 2: words 4 and 8   Sentence 7: words 5 and 3

Sentence 3: words 9 and 2   Sentence 8: words 11 and 6

Sentence 4: words 14 and 6   Sentence 9: words 4, 7, and 9

Sentence 5: words 5 and 15   Sentence 10: words 2, 8, and 7

1. _____

_____

2. _____

_____

3. _____

_____

4. _____

_____

5. _____

_____

6. _____

_____

7. _____

_____

8. _____

_____

9. _____

_____

10. _____

_____

Chapter Thirteen

briskly (227)	bloke (228)	apprehensively (230)	limericks (231)
nondescript (231)	undaunted (233)	absurd (234)	burnished (234)
culprit (235)	roving (236)	twanging (237)	disperse (238)
spitefully (239)	minuscule (242)	blurred (242)	twiddled (243)
feeble (243)	slouched (245)	spiral (245)	furrowed (245)
pursuit (245)	bowled (247)		

Chapter Fourteen

cooped up (249)	squeal (250)	knottiest (250)	hesitant (250)
toadstools (251)	raucous (251)	option (252)	strewn (253)
treading (253)	irresolute (255)	tumultuous (255)	megaphone (256)
swarming (256)	utterly (257)	escorted (257)	retreated (260)
rumpled (260)	recaution (261)	swathed (262)	suspension (263)
cower (263)	admirable (264)	sentiments (264)	

Directions: Make a Book-Go-Round.

1. Cut a piece of 12" X 18" construction paper in half lengthwise. Overlap and paste the two 6" X 18" strips to make one long strip.

2. Pick a vocabulary word and write it on top of the strip. (Check with your teacher to make sure no one else has chosen the same word as you have.)

3. Draw colorful scenes from the book to illustrate the word on the strip.

4. Overlap the two edges and paste them together into a circle. Punch three holes about the same distance apart near the top of the circle.

5. Attach a piece of string to each hole and tie at the top. Hang the Book-Go-Rounds in the classroom.

26

Chapter Fifteen

mullioned (265)	irksome (266)	subdued (268)	prearranged (268)
pruning shears (268)	lagged (269)	buoyant (269)	exasperated (270)
scrawling (270)	brambles (273)	blundered (274)	trundling (274)
craning (275)	specimen (276)	pincered (276)	accelerator (279)
hollow (279)			

Chapter Sixteen

mutinous (284)	subsided (285)	teetering (285)	electrified (286)
ushering (287)	croaky (288)	inkling (289)	Basilisk (290)
aghast (292)	musty (293)	filtering (293)	blanched (294)
bungled (294)	remotely (294)	rammed (296)	disbelievingly (297)
Armenian (297)	harelip (297)	incredulously (297)	slog (298)
hoarsely (302)	mangled (303)	muffled (303)	desperate (304)
pregnant pause (304)	inject (304)	entwined (304)	

Directions: Sort the vocabulary words listed above. You may choose the categories. Here are some suggestions: actions, feelings, descriptive words, words related to places, and words related to appearance.

Chapter Seventeen

serpents (306)	eye sockets (306)	lolled (307)	misted (307)
hoist (308)	broadened (308)	glinted (309)	daubed (310)
suspicious (311)	dispose (311)	coursing (311)	blundering (311)
annoyingly (312)	extraordinary (313)	shimmering (314)	numbly (314)
retorted (315)	talons (315)	shrewdly (315)	frayed (316)
dwindling (316)	suppressed (316)	foul (316)	contorted (317)
numb (317)	slithering (318)	distracted (318)	sabers (318)
thrashed (319)	bulbous (319)	eerie (319)	screwed (319)
contracted (319)	venomous (320)	hilt (320)	drenched (320)
keeled (320)	wrenched (320)	forsaken (321)	spurted (322)
writhing (322)	flailing (322)	bemused (322)	hovering (323)
emitted (324)	placidly (324)	swooped (325)	perplexed (325)
goggled (325)			

Chapter Eighteen

muck (327)	encrusted (328)	rapt (328)	faltered (328)
instinctively (328)	enchant (328)	Albania (328)	consorted (329)
resurfaced (329)	flabbergasted (329)	hoodwinked (330)	daresay (330)
vague (331)	impaled (331)	unaccountably (332)	lurking (332)
quivering (333)	cowering (334)	crouching (334)	abject (334)
disheveled (334)	serenely (335)	prominent (336)	consequences (336)
receding (337)	meddlesome (338)	livid (338)	incensed (338)
cuffing (339)	trifle (339)	sacked (340)	thronging (341)

Directions: Choose 15 vocabulary words from the two lists and write each one in the middle column of the chart. Write an antonym for each word in the left-hand column. Write a synonym for each word in the right-hand column.

Antonym	Vocabulary Word	Synonym

Name _____

Sociogram

Directions: A sociogram shows the relationship between characters in a story. Complete the sociogram below by writing a word to describe the relationship between Harry and each character. Remember, relationships go both ways, so each line requires a descriptive word. Add other characters to the sociogram and describe their relationship with Harry.

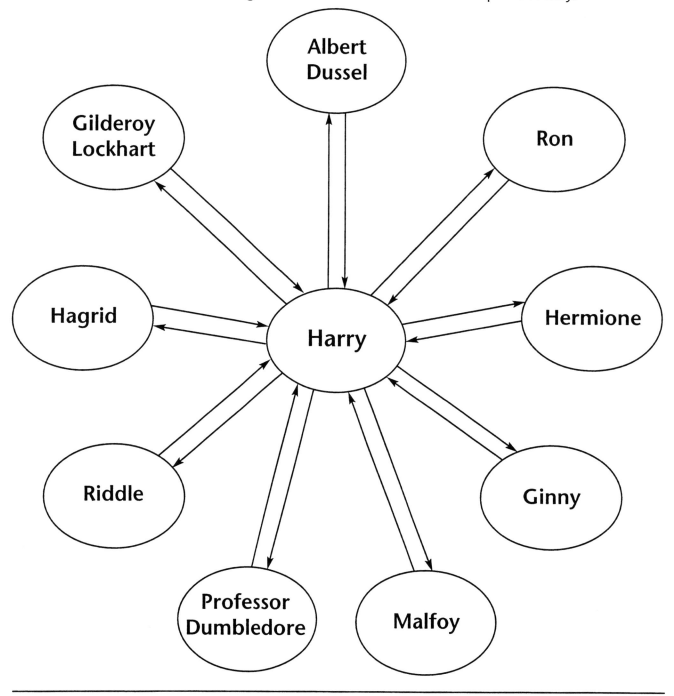

30

Name _____

Conflict

The **conflict** of a story is the struggle between two people or two forces. There are three main types of conflict: person against person, person against nature or society, and person against himself/herself.

Directions: Harry experiences many conflicts during the story. In the chart below, list the names of three characters or forces that Harry must struggle against. In the space provided, list the conflict Harry experiences with each one and explain how each conflict is resolved in the story.

Character:

Conflict	Resolution

Character:

Conflict	Resolution

Character:

Conflict	Resolution

Understanding Values

Directions: Values represent people's beliefs about what is important, good, or worthwhile. For example, most families consider obeying your parents very important— it is something they value.

Think about the following characters from *Harry Potter and the Chamber of Secrets* and the values they have: Harry, Mrs. Weasley, Hermione, Voldemort, Ron, and Hagrid. What do they value? What beliefs do they have about what is important, good, or worthwhile?

On the chart below, list each character's three most important values, from most important to least. Be prepared to share your lists during a class discussion.

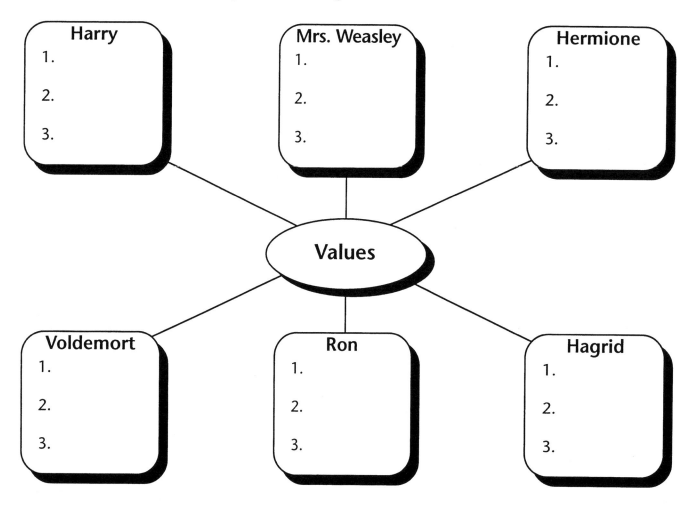

Foreshadowing

Foreshadowing is the literary technique of giving clues to coming events in a story.

Directions: Think about *Harry Potter and the Chamber of Secrets*. What examples of foreshadowing do you recall from the story? If necessary, skim through the chapters to find examples of foreshadowing. List at least four examples below. Explain what clues are given, then list the coming event that is being suggested.

Foreshadowing	Pg. #	Clues	Coming Event

Character Sketch

Directions: Think about the characters from *Harry Potter and the Chamber of Secrets*. Which character was your favorite? Why? List this character's qualities on the attribute web. (You may have made attribute webs for several characters as you read the book. If so, use information recorded from these webs to review the characters and select qualities to list on the attribute web below.) Then use details from the attribute web to write a character sketch of your favorite character.

Acts

1. _____
2. _____
3. _____
4. _____

Feels

1. _____
2. _____
3. _____
4. _____

Character

Looks

1. _____
2. _____
3. _____
4. _____

Says

1. _____
2. _____
3. _____
4. _____

Compare and Contrast

Directions: Think about your school in America and the Hogwart's School in England. In the chart below compare the following: food, language, clothes, weather, holidays, and mode of traveling. How are your parents and Harry's guardians alike? How are they different? In the left-hand column, explain/describe how things are done or how people act at Hogwarts. In the right-hand column, explain/describe how things are done where you go to school.

Hogwarts	My School

Name _____

Newspaper Article

Directions: A well-written newspaper article always answers the journalist's five questions: who? what? when? why? where? In addition, the article usually goes on to explain HOW the events of the story took place. Pretend you are a news reporter for the *Hogwarts News*. Choose one of the following events from *Harry Potter and the Chamber of Secrets* and write an article about it. Remember to answer the journalist's questions and to explain how the events happened. Think of an interesting headline for your article and write it on the top line.

Choose one: Harry and Ron arrive at Hogwarts in the Flying Car. (Chapter 5)
Nearly Headless Nick celebrates his deathday with a party. (Chapter 8)
Harry breaks his arm during the Quidditch Game. (Chapter 10)
Harry rescues Ginny from the Chamber of Secrets. (Chapter 17)

HOGWARTS NEWS

(Insert Headline Here)

_____

_____

_____

_____

_____

_____

_____

_____

_____

_____

_____

Directions: Mark each statement as either True (T) or False (F). If the statement is false, correct it so that it is true.

_____ 1. Harry's twelfth birthday is his best birthday ever.

_____ 2. Dobby warns Harry that he will be in danger if he stays with the Dursleys.

_____ 3. Ron and his brothers use a flying car to help Harry escape from the Dursleys' house.

_____ 4. Harry is very poor and must borrow money from the Weasleys to pay for his schoolbooks.

_____ 5. Harry's favorite way to travel is by Floo powder.

_____ 6. Harry and Ron travel to school in a flying car.

_____ 7. Harry thinks Gilderoy Lockhart is a wise wizard with great ability.

_____ 8. Draco Malfoy places a spell on Ron that causes him to spit up slugs.

_____ 9. Nearly Headless Nick invites Harry to his deathday party.

_____ 10. Harry Petrifies Mrs. Norris as revenge on Filch.

Name _____

Directions: Write a brief (one-two sentences) answer for each question.

1. How was Harry injured during the Quidditch match? Why was he injured?

2. Why did the students think that Harry tried to make the snake attack Justin?

3. What did Harry and Ron discover while under the influence of the Polyjuice potion?

4. What did Harry discover about the Chamber of Secrets by using Tom Riddle's diary?

5. Why did the Minister of Magic take Hagrid away?

6. What did Ron and Harry find out about Hagrid from their trip to the Forbidden Forest?

7. How did Harry find the door to the Chamber of Secrets?

8. Who was held captive in the Chamber of Secrets?

9. Who won the House Cup for the second year running? Why?

Directions: Match the name of the character to the correct quotation. Some names may be used more than once.

A.	Harry Potter
B.	Uncle Vernon
C.	Ron
D.	Dobby
E.	Mr. Weasley
F.	Mrs. Weasley
G.	Gilderoy Lockhart
H.	Draco Malfoy
I.	Professor Dumbledore
J.	Moaning Myrtle
K.	Tom Riddle

_____ 1. "No, no, no. Harry Potter must stay where he is safe. He is too great, too good, to lose. If Harry Potter goes back to Hogwarts, he will be in mortal danger."

_____ 2. "You didn't tell us you weren't allowed to use magic outside school."

_____ 3. "Bless them, they'll go to any lengths to ignore magic, even if it's staring them in the face...But the things our lot have taken to enchanting, you wouldn't believe –"

_____ 4. "He's not even that good, it's just because he's famous...famous for having a stupid scar on his forehead...everyone thinks he's so smart, wonderful Potter with his scar and his broomstick–"

_____ 5. "Of all trees we could've hit, we had to get one that hits back."

_____ 6. "–stealing the car, I wouldn't have been surprised if they'd expelled you, you wait till I get hold of you, I don't suppose you stopped to think what your father and I went through when we saw it was gone–"

_____ 7. "Let me just say that handing out signed pictures at this stage of your career isn't sensible–looks a tad bigheaded, Harry, to be frank."

_____ 8. "I - don't - like - spiders."

_____ 9. "So there is a Chamber of Secrets? And–did you say it's been opened before? Tell me, Dobby!"

_____ 10. "Fascinating creatures, phoenixes. They can carry immensely heavy loads, their tears have healing powers, and they make highly faithful pets."

_____ 11. "However, you will find that I will only truly have left this school when none here are loyal to me. You will also find that help will always be given at Hogwarts to those who ask for it."

_____ 12. "I just remember seeing a pair of great, big, yellow eyes. My whole body sort of seized up, and then I was floating away..."

_____ 13. "Kill the boy! Leave the bird! The boy is behind you! Sniff – Smell him!"

_____ 14. "You shall not harm Harry Potter!"

Directions: Identify each of the following and explain why each one is important in the story.

1. Hogwarts School

2. Moaning Myrtle's bathroom

3. Quidditch

4. Flying car

5. Polyjuice potion

6. Dumbledore's Phoenix

7. Parselmouth

8. Mudbloods

9. Chamber of Secrets

10. Floo powder

11. Muggles

12. Sorting Hat

Directions: Circle the letter for the BEST answer to each question.

1. What was the sport that Harry missed more than anything else at Hogwarts?
   A. soccer
   B. Quidditch
   C. baseball
   D. football

2. Who came to warn Harry not to go back to Hogwarts?
   A. Uncle Vernon
   B. Draco Malfoy
   C. Dudley
   D. Dobby

3. How did Harry escape his room in order to visit Ron Weasley during summer break?
   A. He climbed out of his window and slid down a rope.
   B. Dobby helped him unlock the door while the Masons were eating dinner with the Dursleys.
   C. Ron brought a flying car up to Harry's bedroom window so he could climb out and fly away.
   D. Mr. and Mrs. Dursley were so mad at Harry that they kicked him out of the house.

4. Why was Ron embarrassed about bringing Harry to visit his home?
   A. The Weasleys were poor and did not have an expensive house.
   B. Ron's sister, Ginny, was a pest and would make fun of Harry.
   C. Mr. and Mrs. Weasley did not like visitors.
   D. The ghoul in the attic would disturb Harry by turning on and off the lights during the night.

5. What was the most unusual thing that Harry noticed about the Weasley household?
   A. The Weasley family had a talking mirror and ghouls in the attic.
   B. Everybody in the Weasley family really liked Harry.
   C. The Weasleys always complained about being poor.
   D. Mr. and Mrs. Weasley were very strict and mean.

6. What happened to Harry when he took a pinch of Floo powder to be transported to Diagon Alley?
   A. He ended up in an old castle that was haunted by ghosts.
   B. Harry was flown to his bedroom at the Dursleys' house.
   C. Harry landed at Mr. Gorgin's dark magic shop, fell on his face, and broke his glasses.
   D. Harry missed Diagon Alley but reached the elephant's cage at the zoo.

7. Why did Ron and Harry miss the train to Hogwarts?
    A. The boys couldn't get through the barrier to the platform nine and three-quarters.
    B. Mr. Wesley's flying car broke down and they were too late to catch the train.
    C. Harry forgot his owl, Hedwig, at the Weasleys' house and had to go back to get it.
    D. Malfoy saw Harry at the station and threatened Harry with a beating if he got on the train.

8. How did Ron and Harry finally get to Hogwarts?
    A. They crashed through the barrier with their trolleys and flagged the Hogwarts' train down.
    B. Mr. and Mrs. Dursley drove the boys to Hogwarts in their new car.
    C. Dumbledore waved his magic wand and transported the boys to the Hogwarts' main hall.
    D. Ron stole his father's flying car to take Harry and himself to Hogwarts.

9. Gilderoy Lockhart could be described as
    A. a smiling, turquois-robed, incompetent professor
    B. the Professor of the Magic Wand Arts at Hogwarts
    C. a true friend of Harry and Ron who saves them from Riddle
    D. a ghost at Hogwarts who haunts the girls' bathroom

10. Some of the students at Hogwarts were called Mudbloods because
    A. they kept their rooms clean
    B. they got muddy when they played Quidditch in the rain
    C. their parents did not have magic powers
    D. their blood was the color of mud

11. Who had his five hundredth deathday party on Halloween?
    A. Nearly Headless Nick
    B. Filch and Mrs. Norris
    C. Peeves
    D. Malfoy

12. What happened to Argus Filch's cat?
    A. It was run over by Ron's flying car.
    B. It was Petrified by a mysterious villain.
    C. The cat was eaten by Hagrid's friend, the giant spider.
    D. It ran away because she did not like the food at Hogwarts.

42

13. Why does Hermione want Professor Lockhart to sign the note for the restricted sections of the library?
    A. Hermione needs to do some background reading for the Professor's class.
    B. The restricted book she wants has the recipe for the potion that transforms people into other forms.
    C. Hermione really likes Professor Lockhart and wants to keep the note because it has his autograph on it.
    D. Ron and Harry want to make a magic potion that will change Malfoy into a rat.

14. Where do Ron, Hermione, and Harry hide in order to make the Polyjuice potion?
    A. in the Gryffindor hall
    B. in the deep forest outside Hogwarts
    C. at the small house of Hagrid's
    D. in Moaning Myrtle's bathroom

15. Who conducted the dueling club?
    A. Professor Dumbledore
    B. Professor Snape
    C. Professor Lockhart
    D. Malfoy

16. Why was Harry called Parselmouth?
    A. Harry could speak to and understand what snakes said.
    B. Harry's mouth was changed into the shape of a parcel package.
    C. Harry could speak very softly like the hiss of dragons.
    D. Harry liked to eat the cookies that came through the parcel post.

17. What did Hermione turn into when she drank the Polyjuice potion?
    A. Millicent Bulstrode
    B. a cat
    C. Goyle
    D. Crabbe

18. The secret entrance to the Chamber of Secrets was
    A. through the portrait in the Gryffindor Hall
    B. at the entrance to the dungeon
    C. in the cave of the monstrous spiders
    D. in a sink in Moaning Myrtle's bathroom

19. Who was captured and taken down into the serpent's cave?
    A. Harry
    B. Ron
    C. Ginny
    D. Riddle

20. Who saved Harry from the gigantic Basilisk's killing stare?
    A. Dumbledore's Phoenix
    B. Malfoy
    C. Ginny
    D. Gilderoy

I. Analysis (Choose A or B)

A. Think about Harry, the main character from the story. How does Harry change during the story? Does he change for the better or the worse? Write a composition (two paragraphs minimum) that explains how Harry changes and whether these changes are for the better or the worse. Use information from the story to support your answer.

B. Think about events that happen in *Harry Potter and the Chamber of Secrets*. How does one event sometimes cause another? Choose an event from the story and write a brief composition (one to two paragraphs) that explains how this event caused the others to happen. Use information from the story to support your answer.

II. Creative Writing (Choose A or B)

A. Pretend that you are Harry. Write five journal entries about some of the events that happen to you at Hogwarts School.

B. Dumbledore tells Harry, "It is our choices, Harry, that show what we truly are, far more than our abilities." What does Dumbledore mean? Write a poem about people (mothers, fathers, aunts, uncles, grandparents, guardians, friends, etc.) who have made difficult choices and how those choices affected someone's life in a positive way.

Answer Key

Activities #1 and #2: Answers will vary

Study Questions—Chapter One: 1. "You've forgotten the magic word." 2. Hogwarts School of Witchcraft and Wizardry 3. He misses the castle, mail arriving by owl, eating banquets, sleeping in the four-poster bed, visiting the gamekeeper, and playing Quidditch 4. A lightening-shaped scar 5. Stay in his room, make no noise, and pretend he is not there 6. Buy a vacation home in Majorca 7. He has never felt so lonely. 8. Hedwig is locked in a cage and Harry is not allowed to use his powers outside of school. 9. Two huge, green eyes staring at him 10. Mrs. Dursley tries to hit Harry with a frying pan then puts him to work all day without food until he is finished. 11. Two slices of bread and a lump of cheese

Chapter Two: 1. Dobby 2. Large, bat-like ears and bulging, green eyes the size of tennis balls 3. An old pillowcase 4. A house-elf 5. Dobby begins to cry. 6. Dobby warns Harry not to go back to Hogwarts. 7. Dobby intercepted them. 8. He uses a spell to ruin Mrs. Dursley's dessert, and then the Ministry of Magic sends Harry a letter warning him not to cast any spells outside of school. 9. Via owl 10. The letter from the Ministry of Magic states that Harry can't practice magic outside of school. 11. He locks Harry in his room. 12. He dreams he is on display at a zoo. 13. Ron Weasley

Chapter Three: 1. A flying car 2. Ron's dad works for the Ministry. 3. Ron's brothers pick the lock on Harry's door and sneaks downstairs to get Harry's stuff. 4. Harry forgets Hedwig, so she screeches and wakes Mr. Dursley. 5. Ron, Fred, and George pull on Harry's arms as they speed away in the car and Harry finally slips from Mr. Dursley's grasp. 6. He wants to give Hedwig a chance to fly because she has been stuck in the cage all summer. 7. "See you next summer!" 8. Draco Malfoy's father; he supports "You-Know-Who" 9. Ron's delivery owl 10. The Misuse of Muggle Artifacts Office 11. She scolds them. 12. Ron's little sister Ginny 13. De-gnome it 14. "Gerroff me!" 15. A few shrinking door keys and a biting kettle

Chapter Four: 1. "Tuck your shirt in, scruffy!" 2. Everyone seems to like Harry. 3. Eat four helpings at every meal. 4. Gilderoy Lockhart 5. Errol the owl 6. Schoolwork 7. Charlie is in Romania studying dragons and Bill is in Egypt working for the wizard's bank, Gringotts. 8. By using Floo powder 9. Draco Malfoy 10. Hagrid 11. Flesh-Eating Slug Repellent 12. Small, goblin-driven carts that speed along miniature train tracks through the bank's underground tunnels 13. "Prefects Who Gained Power" 14. He is going to be the new Defense Against the Dark Arts teacher at Hogwarts School. He is also giving Harry free copies of his books. 15. He tells Ginny she can have them, then puts them in her cauldron. 16. Lucius Malfoy; Hagrid

Chapter Five: 1. They set off their Filibuster fireworks. 2. Mr. Weasley added special features to make the trunk magically expand. 3. You have to walk through the solid barrier that divides platform nine and ten without any Muggles seeing you do it. 4. They can't get through the barrier to platform nine and three-quarters. 5. They use the flying car. 6. Ron's parents can apparate. 7. No. They land in a tree. 8. It attacks the car. 9. The sorting ceremony is taking place. 10. Several Muggles saw the flying car. 11. Send a letter by owl 12. Detention and a letter home to their families 13. Wattlebird

Chapter Six: 1. It is a verbal scolding sent via letter. 2. Ron receives the Howler from his mother. It scolds him for taking the car and getting his father into trouble. 3. They just finished doctoring the tree Ron and Harry crashed into. 4. He tells Harry to calm down, that there will be plenty of time to get noticed when Harry is older. 5. It is used to return people who have been transfigured or cursed to their original state. 6. The cry of the Mandrake is fatal to anyone who hears it. 7. Take a picture of Harry and sign it. 8. Lockhart offers to let Colin take a picture of him posing with Harry and offers to have both of them sign it. 9. To rid the world of evil and market his own range of hair-care potions. 10. The pixies wreak havoc on the class.

Chapter Seven: 1. It goes out of control and hits the teacher in the face. 2. He explains how to play Quidditch. 3. Seeker 4. The Slytherin team 5. Draco Malfoy 6. New Nimbus Two Thousand and One brooms 7. Green slugs 8. Hagrid's house 9. Gilderoy Lockhart 10. Someone who is Muggle-born or has non-magic parents 11. Giant pumpkins 12. Ron is to polish silver in the trophy room and Harry is to help Lockhart answer his fan mail. 13. He hears a voice threaten him.

Chapter Eight: 1. Nearly Headless Nick 2. Argus Filch 3. The school poltergeist that likes to wreak havoc and cause distress 4. A letter advertising a Kwickspell course. 5. Nearly Headless Nick 6. His five hundredth deathday party 7. The girl's bathroom 8. It was all rotten and smelly 9. He isn't pale like the other ghosts, and is wearing a bright orange party hat, revolving bow tie, and a broad grin. 10. The same evil voice he heard in Lockhart's office 11. Mrs. Norris the cat

Chapter Nine: 1. He becomes very upset and accuses Harry of killing Mrs. Norris. 2. No 3. Transmogrifian Torture 4. A potion made from the Mandrakes 5. By taking Harry off the Quidditch team 6. A person born into a wizarding family but who has no magical powers 7. She is a cat lover. 8. She wants to learn more about the Chamber of Secrets. 9. Professor Binns 10. A monster that only the Heir of Slytherin can control 11. Harry 12. Spiders 13. Moaning Myrtle 14. Draco Malfoy 15. A potion that transforms you into somebody else.

Chapter Ten: 1. Gilderoy Lockhart 2. Moaning Myrtle's bathroom 3. Powdered horn of a bicorn, shredded skin of a boomslang, and a bit of whatever they want to change into 4. Threatening Muggle-borns 5. About one month 6. Scarlet 7. A Bludger 8. The Bludger hits him. 9. Lockhart 10. The spell doesn't mend Harry's broken arm; it removes the bones. 11. It painfully regrows the bones in his arm and hands. 12. Dobby 13. Dobby 14. Colin Peevey; he has been Petrified

Chapter Eleven: 1. Moaning Myrtle's bathroom 2. They take turns covering themselves with boils or fur and jumping out at her from behind statues. 3. Use the Polyjuice potion to get Malfoy to admit he is the Heir to Slytherin 4. Put one of Fred's Filibuster fireworks in Goyle's cauldron 5. Lockhart and Snape 6. Wands 7. Malfoy 8. The ability to speak to snakes 9. The ability to speak Parselmouth 10. They suspect Harry is a dark wizard. 11. Justin and Nearly Headless Nick

Chapter Twelve: 1. The Sorting Hat 2. He would have done well in Slytherin. 3. A phoenix 4. Carry immensely heavy loads, their tears have healing powers, and they make highly faithful pets 5. No 6. Ron thinks Malfoy is responsible for all the attacks and is mad that Harry is getting all the credit. 7. They visit Bill in Egypt 8. A toothpick and a note asking if he will be staying at Hogwarts during summer vacation too. 9. Millicent Bulstrode 10. One hour 11. Overcooked cabbage, the khaki color of a booger 12. Pure-blood 13. A newspaper clipping about Ron's father getting fined because of the flying car 14. The Wizard prison

Chapter Thirteen: 1. To shield her from view to spare her the embarrassment of being seen with a fury face 2. Gilderoy Lockhart 3. Someone threw a book at her. 4. Fifty years old 5. T. M. Riddle 6. He bought the diary from Vauxhall Road. 7. Caught the Heir of Slytherin 8. They are becoming moody and secretive. 9. Valentine celebration complete with ugly decorations and cupids delivering messages 10. Draco Malfoy 11. All his books have red ink on them except for the diary. 12. He writes in the diary and the diary writes back. 13. Tom's father is a Muggle and his mother died right after he was born. 14. Hagrid

Chapter Fourteen: 1. Hagrid's three-headed dog 2. Ron, Harry, and Hermione decide not to talk to Hagrid unless there is another attack. 3. They will be fully mature when they try to move into each other's pots. 4. Quidditch 5. Tom Riddle's diary 6. Hermione and a girl from Ravenclaw 7. A mirror 8. An Invisibility cloak 9. They use Mr. Potter's cloak. 10. Dumbledore, Cornelius Fudge, and Lucius Malfoy 11. To Azkaban 12. No 13. Dumbledore has been suspended as headmaster. 14. The Muggle-borns won't have a chance and there will be a killing. 15. To follow the spiders

Chapter Fifteen: 1. He finds it irksome. 2. Draco Malfoy 3. Professor Snape 4. To the Forbidden Forest 5. Unicorns and Centaurs 6. From six o'clock on, the Gryffindors had no place to go and everyone was talking about what was happening at Hogwarts. 7. There is no need for it in the pitch-dark forest. 8. His wand lights up like a flashlight. Ron is afraid his wand will blow up. 9. It acts like a dog greeting its owner. 10. The spider friend of Hagrid who was accused of the attacks at Hogwarts fifty years earlier 11. Out of respect for Hagrid 12. A distant land 13. The flying car rescues them. 14. He always thinks monsters aren't as bad as they're made out to be. 15. Moaning Myrtle

Chapter Sixteen: 1. Professor McGonagall 2. She announces that the Mandrakes are ready for cutting and can be used to revive the Petrified people. 3. Ginny 4. Percy 5. Professor McGonagall 6. They tell her they are going to see Hermione in the hospital. 7. He finds a page from a library book with information on the Basilisk. 8. He sees the word "pipes" written on the paper. 9. Only Harry can understand Parseltongue. 10. Spiders run away. 11. The Basilisk moves through the plumbing pipes. 12. They are going to the staff room because she has a break in ten minutes. 13. They hide in the teacher's wardrobe. 14. She tells them that the monster has taken Ginny Weasley. 15. Professor Gilderoy Lockhart 16. They think Lockhart will help them. 17. Lockhart is packing his bags to run away from the castle. 18. No, he makes up his brave deeds. 19. She tells him that she saw two great, big, yellow eyes. 20. He talks Parseltongue. 21. He will tell them that it was too late to save the girl and that the two boys lost their minds when they saw her mangled body. 22. The wand explodes and sends a rock wall tumbling down between Ron and Harry. 23. Harry continues on into the tunnel in order to find and rescue Ginny from the monster.

Chapter Seventeen: 1. He thinks that the Basilisk might be lurking in a shadowy corner and he wonders about where Ginny might be. 2. He sees a statue as high as the chamber that has a monkeyish face and a long beard. 3. Tom looked about sixteen years old with a weird, misty light shinning about him. 4. Tom tells Harry that he is a memory that is preserved in a diary for fifty years. 5. Ginny wrote that her brothers tease her, she had to come to school with second hand books, and she wanted Harry to like her. 6. She became suspicious of the diary. 7. Professor Dumbledore sees through Tom's frame of Hagrid. 8. Tom wants Harry to answer the question: "How did you escape with nothing but a scar, while Lord Voldemort's powers were destroyed?" 9. Tom Riddle says that he is Lord Voldemort. 10. He hears eerie, spine-tingling, unearthly music coming from somewhere. 11. A crimson bird the size of a swan with a glittering golden tail and gleaming golden talons 12. The bird landed on Harry's shoulder. 13. The bird dropped the old school Sorting Hat at Harry's feet. 14. Harry's mother died to save Harry from Voldemort. 15. Tom wants to match his powers with the best weapons that Dumbledore has sent to Harry. 16. They are both half-bloods, orphans, and can speak Parseltongue. 17. A gigantic serpent uncoiled itself from Slytherin's mouth. 18. The phoenix attacks the Basilisk. 19. The phoenix punctures the eyes of the Basilisk. 20. A gleaming silver sword with a handle glittering with rubies falls out of the hat. 21. Fawkes cries tears on Harry's wound. 22. Harry pierces the diary with the fang of the Basilisk. 23 Ginny awakes and begins to cry. 24. The Memory Charm backfired and he looses his memory. 25. Fawkes, the phoenix, flies them up through the tunnel.

Chapter Eighteen: 1. Mrs. Weasley is crying because she thinks that Ginny is dead. 2. Fawkes flies to Dumbledore's shoulder. 3. Tom's diary that was written when Riddle was sixteen years old 4. Ginny found the diary inside one of the books her mother had bought her. 5. Dumbledore tells the students that the Petrified victims have no lasting harm done to them. 6. Her first name is Minerva. 7. No, he does not expel them. 8. No, because the Memory Charm backfired. 9. Ron takes Lockhart up to the infirmary. 10. Dumbledore thanks Harry. 11. Lord Voldemort transferred some of his powers to Harry the night Harry got the scar from Lord Voldemort's wand. 12. Harry's choices make him different. 13. Dumbledore says only a true Gryffindor could have pulled the sword from the Sorting Hat. 14. Dumbledore says that Harry needs food and sleep. 15. Lucius Malfoy comes barging into the office. 16. Dobby, the servant of Malfoy 17. Dobby is pointing to the diary and Malfoy. 18. Lucius Malfoy hid the book inside one of Ginny's textbooks. 19. Harry slips the diary into one of his smelly

---

© Novel Units, Inc.

47

socks and hands it to Malfoy. 20. Dobby is set free and is no longer Malfoy's servant. 21. Harry asks Dobby not to try to save his life again. 22. Most of the teachers cheered. 23. Percy was kissing his new girlfriend. 24. Harry asked Ron to telephone him during the summer.

Activities #3 through #21: Answers will vary.

Comprehension Quiz 1
1.F 2.F 3.T 4.F 5.F 6.T 7.F 8.F 9.T 10.F
Comprehension Quiz 2
1. Dobby placed a spell on the Bludger to make it attack Harry. The Bludger hits Harry and breaks his arm. 2. The students cannot speak Parselmouth, so to them it looked like Harry was urging the snake to attack Justin. 3. Ron's father was fined fifty gold Galleons because of the flying car and Draco Malfoy doesn't know who the Heir of Slytherin is. 4. Tom exposed Hagrid as the one who opened the Chamber of Secrets. 5. Under pressure to take action, the Minister of Magic focuses on Hagrid because Hagrid was blamed for the attacks fifty years earlier. 6. Hagrid was not responsible for opening the Chamber of Secrets fifty years earlier. 7. He talks to Moaning Myrtle in the girl's bathroom and discovers that she died because she looked into the Basilisk's eyes. He then guesses that the door is somewhere in the bathroom. He finds a symbol of a serpent on a faucet and uses Parseltongue to get it to open the door to the Chamber of Secrets. 8. Ginny Weasley 9. Gryffindor won the cup because Harry and Ron earned 400 points for their House by rescuing Ginny from the Basilisk.

Novel Tests
Quotations: 1.D (p. 16) 2.B (p. 21) 3.E (p. 38) 4.H (p. 50) 5.C (p. 76) 6.E (p. 88) 7.G (p. 98) 8.C (p. 154) 9.A (p. 178) 10.I (p. 207) 11.I (p. 263) 12.J (p. 299) 13.K (p. 320) 14.D (p. 338)
Identification: Answers will vary.
Multiple Choice: 1.B 2.D 3.C 4.A 5.B 6.C 7.A 8.D 9.A 10.C 11.A 12.B 13.B 14.D 15.C 16.A 17.B 18.D 19.C 20.A
Essays: Answers will vary.